MN

MIGHTY MACHINES

Skid Steer Loaders

by Kay Manolis

BLASTOFF! READERS

BELLWETHER MEDIA · MINNEAPOLIS, MN

Note to Librarians, Teachers, and Parents:

Blastoff! Readers are carefully developed by literacy experts and combine standards-based content with developmentally appropriate text.

Level 1 provides the most support through repetition of high-frequency words, light text, predictable sentence patterns, and strong visual support.

Level 2 offers early readers a bit more challenge through varied simple sentences, increased text load, and less repetition of high-frequency words.

Level 3 advances early-fluent readers toward fluency through increased text and concept load, less reliance on visuals, longer sentences, and more literary language.

Level 4 builds reading stamina by providing more text per page, increased use of punctuation, greater variation in sentence patterns, and increasingly challenging vocabulary.

Level 5 encourages children to move from "learning to read" to "reading to learn" by providing even more text, varied writing styles, and less familiar topics.

Whichever book is right for your reader, Blastoff! Readers are the perfect books to build confidence and encourage a love of reading that will last a lifetime!

This edition first published in 2009 by Bellwether Media.

No part of this publication may be reproduced in whole or in part without written permission of the publisher. For information regarding permission, write to Bellwether Media Inc., Attention: Permissions Department, Post Office Box 19349, Minneapolis, MN 55419.

Library of Congress Cataloging-in-Publication Data
Manolis, Kay.
  Skid steer loaders / by Kay Manolis.
    p. cm. — (Blastoff! readers. Mighty machines)
  Summary: "Simple text and full color photographs introduce young readers to skid steer loaders. Intended for students in kindergarten through third grade"—Provided by publisher.
  Includes bibliographical references and index.
  ISBN-13: 978-1-60014-181-2 (hardcover : alk. paper)
  ISBN-10: 1-60014-181-1 (hardcover : alk. paper)
  1. Loaders (Machines)—Juvenile literature. 2. Excavating machinery—Juvenile literature. 3. Earthmoving machinery—Juvenile literature. I. Title.

TA725.M325 2009
621.8'6—dc22   2008012233

Contents

A skid steer loader is a construction machine. It can do many jobs.

A skid steer loader can work in small spaces.

Skid steer
loaders have
a **cab**.
The driver
sits in the cab.

cab

The driver uses **control sticks**. These move the skid steer loader.

control sticks

Skid steer loaders can use many tools. This one has an **auger**. It digs holes.

auger

This skid steer loader has a **bucket**. It moves heavy rocks or dirt.

bucket

This skid steer loader has a **jackhammer**. It breaks up the ground.

jackhammer

This skid steer
loader has
a **fork**.
It moves trees.

fork

This skid steer loader moves hay. Good work!

Glossary

auger—a sharp tool that spins to dig holes

bucket—a part of a machine that can lift, scoop, carry, and dump heavy objects

cab—a place where the driver sits

control sticks—the rods a driver uses to move a skid steer loader

fork—a group of sharp metal bars that can lift and carry heavy objects

jackhammer—a sharp metal tool that can break up concrete or rock

To Learn More

AT THE LIBRARY

Hoban, Tana. *Construction Zone*. New York: Greenwillow, 1997.

Palotta, Jerry. *The Construction Alphabet Book*. Watertown, Mass.: Charlesbridge, 2006.

Richards, Jon. *Diggers and Other Construction Machines*. Brookfield, Conn.: Milbrook Press, 1999.

ON THE WEB

Learning more about mighty machines is as easy as 1, 2, 3.

1. Go to www.factsurfer.com

2. Enter "mighty machines" into search box.

3. Click the "Surf" button and you will see a list of related web sites.

With factsurfer.com, finding more information is just a click away.

Index

The images in this book are reproduced through the courtesy of: Gualberto Becerra, front cover; Deere, Inc., pp. 5, 7, 9, 11, 13, 15, 17, 19, 21.